A New Hearing Of An Old Prayer

Sermons On The Lord's Prayer

Thomas C. Short

CSS Publishing Company, Inc.
Lima, Ohio

A NEW HEARING OF AN OLD PRAYER

Copyright © 1995 by
CSS Publishing Company, Inc.
Lima, Ohio

All rights reserved. No part of this publication may be reproduced, stored in a retrieval system, or transmitted in any form or by any means, electronic, mechanical, photocopying, recording, or otherwise, without the prior permission of the publisher. Inquiries should be addressed to: CSS Publishing Company, Inc., 517 South Main Street, P.O. Box 4503, Lima, Ohio 45802-4503.

Library of Congress Cataloging-in-Publication Data

Short, Thomas C., 1936-
    A new hearing of an old prayer : sermons on the Lord's Prayer / Thomas C. Short.
    p.   cm.
    Includes bibliographical references.
    ISBN 0-7880-0323-2
    1. Lord's prayer — Sermons. 2. Eastertide — Sermons. 3. Sermons, American.
I. Title.
BV230.S424   1995
226.9'606—dc   94-35868
                                                                                 CIP

This book is available in the following formats, listed by ISBN:
0-7880-0323-2 Book

PRINTED IN U.S.A.

*This book is dedicated
to my wife Mary,
who prays with me
and for me*

It is with a sense of pride and fulfillment that CSS Publishing Company launches the Great American Preacher Series. One of two initial releases, this volume epitomizes the kind of quality writing, scholarship and practicality which have shaped the foundation of CSS preaching resources for nearly three decades.

Written by some of America's best contemporary preachers, this series promises to inspire you with fresh insights into the timeless message of the Gospel; provide models of excellence for sermon creation; deal respectfully and sensitively with the Word of God; spark your own imagination and creativity with outline and illustration possibilities; and minister to you personally as you continue to grow in your relationship with God and others.

CSS Publishing Company considers it a privilege to introduce this series into your preaching, study and reading disciplines. With additional volumes planned in the future, we invite you to become a regular participant in this adventure of shared ideas.

Table Of Contents

Introduction	7
Foreword	9
The Easter Entry	11
Two Images Of The Father	17
Hallowed Be Thy Name	25
Thy Kingdom Come, Thy Will Be Done On Earth As It Is In Heaven	33
Give Us This Day Our Daily Bread	41
Forgive Us As We Forgive Others	49
Lead Us Not Into Temptation But Deliver Us From Evil	57

Introduction

We live in a strange time. Many statistics show that more people claim to have a deeper religious faith, but at the same time, fewer people in our society know the words to the Lord's Prayer. I have noticed this when small groups are gathered together for weddings and funerals. One of my colleagues prints the words of the Lord's Prayer in the Sunday worship bulletin each week because so many people don't know it by memory.

Years ago every child, "churched" and "unchurched," learned the words of this prayer in the public schools, but that is no longer the case. If you are not in a church-related school or in a church family, the possibilities of you learning the words of the Lord's Prayer are remote. That is shocking news to those of us who have known and said the prayer through the years. From my experience, it is the only prayer that we can even attempt to say from memory in congregational settings.

While I regret the "loss" of this prayer from the public domain, I also issue a word of warning to myself and others who know it and love it. There is the possibility that we are so familiar with the words of the prayer that we say it with little meaning or understanding. Have we become so familiar with it that we "repeat" it rather than "pray" it? People have confided in me that their minds often "wander" when the congregation prays the prayer. If we are not careful, we'll just stand up and say it with little or no meaning or understanding.

For these and other reasons I led my congregation in the following study of our Lord's prayer, and I was amazed at their interest and appreciation. They were hungry for each new phrase. I print copies of my Sunday sermons for members of the congregation and we had to increase significantly the number of copies during this series. Through this experience, many of us learned that this prayer is so familiar that we sometimes take its words and thoughts for granted.

Consequently, I invite you to study the Lord's Prayer with me in the following chapters. Since this series is designed to begin on Easter Sunday, I will begin the study with the concluding words of the prayer ("for thine is the kingdom and the power and the glory") which I call the "Easter Entry." This is a phrase which was added by our ancestors, adopted by much of the Christian Church and made a part of the prayer.

Foreword

Prayer is communion with God. Augustine said, "For thee were we made, O God, and our hearts are restless until they find their rest in thee." The psalmist chose these words to express the same thought: "O God, thou art my God, I see thee, my soul thirsts for thee; my flesh faints for thee, as in a dry and weary land where no water is" (Psalm 63:1).

Prayer is the coming together of two who belong together. Since prayer is the union of the created and the creator, the result of prayer is not reward but relationship. It is "deep" crying unto the "deep." Remember Florence Allshorn's simple prayer, "O God, here am I and here are You." Prayer is communion. It is one of the ways we have of moving toward the God for whom we thirst.

Obviously, such a communion includes times of silence, times for listening. Jesus cautioned his followers about exhausting their prayer time with talk when he reminded them that the heathens thought "they (would) be heard for their many words" (Matthew 6:7). Martin Luther felt so strongly about this that he taught, "The fewer the words, the better the prayer."

John Greenleaf Whittier put this thought in verse:

O Sabbath rest by Galilee, O calm of hills above,
where Jesus knelt to share with thee
the silence of eternity, interpreted by love.

Were not these the thoughts of the Psalmist when he wrote: "He leads me beside the still waters. He restores my soul" (Psalm 23:2-3)? Frequently, the soul is restored more in the quietness beside the still waters than in the jungle of words. Leslie Weatherhead gives us one man's testimony in his book, *The Christian Agnostic*. This man had told Dr. Weatherhead, "Again and again, a quiet, solitary, wordless walk by the sea-shore with my heart deeply grateful for all his love and mercy; a heart opened to him in adoration and quietly receptive to the impact of his spirit, has meant far more than any prayer meeting or list of petitions, or any verbal confession, or any wordy prayer, for in such an experience the relationship with God is restored and freshened ..." (p. 221).

Taking the time for silence, for listening is certainly a part of prayer, but talking is also a part of it. There is a time to talk. There is a time to speak. There is very little communion with God if we don't take the time to listen, but the same is true if we do not talk.

This is not a new idea. What is your earliest memory of prayer? Didn't you talk to God? As a little child you may have knelt beside the bed and said, "Now I lay me down to sleep. I pray the Lord my soul to keep." Then you blessed Mommy and Daddy, brothers and sisters, aunts and uncles, dogs and cats and most of the other creatures of the earth. Words! You used words! You talked to the Lord.

Consequently, the same Jesus who taught us not to be too wordy, also gave us words for a prayer. Through the years these words have become known as the Lord's Prayer. Along with millions of other people you and I have learned this prayer, and consequently, it serves as a wonderful vehicle for corporate prayer.

In the United Methodist service for marriage, the congregation is invited to pray together after the pronouncement of the marriage. It's a very moving part of the service. After I have pronounced the couple husband and wife, I say, "Now, as their first act together as husband and wife, Mr. and Mrs. (name) invite you to pray with them our Lord's Prayer." And the family members and guests fill the room with their voices as we say together our Lord's Prayer. Words. Wonderful words. In our communion with God, there is a time to talk.

It's a joy to join with you in the study of this prayer and through this journey together to discover some of the deeper meanings of our Lord's words.

Thomas C. Short

A Prayer Of Confession

O God of might and mystery,
  we confess that we sometimes have difficulty
  accepting the resurrection of Jesus from the dead.
We pride ourselves on being reasonable people,
  and his resurrection is beyond our reasoning abilities.
We build our lives around logic and knowledge,
  and we can neither explain nor understand
  Jesus' resurrection.
O God, pour your grace into our academic minds
  and your love into our hardened hearts.
Touch us with a power
  that raises us above logic and knowledge.
In the name of our risen Christ, we pray. Amen.

Our Lord's Prayer

The Easter Entry

"For thine is the kingdom and the power and the glory forever." That's how our Lord's prayer ends. Oddly enough these are the only words in the prayer that Jesus did not teach us to pray. Most scholars agree that these closing words to the prayer were added later by the followers of Jesus. Consequently, they are not a part of the biblical text, the Lord's Prayer, as taught by Jesus. Even as children we knew there was something different about this line in the prayer.

When our Roman Catholic friends say this prayer, which they call the "Our Father," they do not include this last line. They pray only the prayer as taught by Jesus and recorded in the scriptures. So their prayer ends with the words "lead us not into temptation but deliver us from evil." If you are visiting in a Roman Catholic church and say, "For thine is the kingdom and the power and the glory forever," you say these words by yourself.

Does it really matter to you that these words were not given to us by Jesus? Isn't it a beautiful thing that his followers put this ending to his prayer? You might know the story of Mozart who was commissioned to write a requiem Mass for the people of Vienna. Even though he was a very sick man he worked diligently on the opening movement. His lungs became more and more congested and his coughing spasms grew more severe. Shortly after writing the "Lachrymosa" passage, he died. His work was unfinished, but his students could not bear to have it remain incomplete. They could not let this masterpiece go unfinished and unsung. So the students studied Mozart's work and his techniques and movements and they completed the Mass. Wherever that *Requiem* is sung today it brings honor to the original composer, Mozart. And so it is with the final line in our Lord's prayer. When we say, "For thine is the kingdom and the power and the glory forever," we are honoring the Christ who gave us the prayer.

But why did his followers add this line? What great event caused them to make this addition? I suggest to you that they added it because God raised up Christ from the dead. It is the Easter Entry to our Lord's prayer. After their crucified Christ was raised up from the dead, his followers believed with all their hearts "thine is the kingdom and the power and the glory forever." So they wrote this line of praise, this doxology, this Easter Entry. It was the most natural conclusion to His prayer.

In Matthew's account of the Easter story, we read these words: "An angel of the Lord descended from heaven, and came and rolled back the stone from the door and sat on it" (28:2b). Isn't that an incredible line! What an image! The angel of God rolled the stone away from the tomb and sat upon it. God reigned over all: the stone, the tomb and even death. When the followers of Jesus experienced this great work of God they wrote: "Thine is the kingdom and the power and the glory for ever." It's the Easter Entry.

It is a summary of Paul's great proclamation to the church at Corinth when he wrote, "Death is swallowed up in victory. O death, where is thy victory? O death, where is thy sting? ... thanks be to God, who gives us the victory through our

Lord Jesus Christ" (1 Corinthians 15:54-57). Yes, "thine is the kingdom and the power and the glory for ever." It's the Easter Entry.

Can't you sense this feeling in the lives of the women who went to anoint the body of Jesus? They were reasonable people. Someone had to anoint the body for burial and they were answering the call to duty. As they knifed their way through the morning darkness they discussed the barriers that might stand in their way. After all, who would roll the stone away? That was a reasonable question. And these were reasonable women, addressing reasonable questions. When they got to the tomb and saw that the stone had been rolled away and the body was missing, they immediately came to a reasonable conclusion. Someone had stolen the body of Jesus. Doesn't that make sense? Some of the women ran to tell the disciples what had happened: namely, that the body was missing and someone had stolen it. They were perfectly reasonable. They were too reasonable to think of resurrection. Jesus had talked about it but they had not really heard him. Others ran to the tomb but none seemed to grasp the good news of resurrection.

One by one they left the tomb, but Mary lingered behind. She saw the risen Christ and thought him to be a gardener. Isn't that what happens when you see one whom you do not expect to see? It must be someone else. She thought like that because resurrection was not a possibility in her mind. That was too other-worldly, too incredible, too unreasonable, too out of her control.

Then Jesus spoke to her and she recognized him. She called him "Teacher." It was He. Bigger than life it was Jesus. She was seeing what she had least expected to see. She was experiencing what she least expected to experience. Resurrection! At that moment there was only one thing for her to conclude. God really did have the final word. It was true. God reigned even over death. Out of this experience the followers added the closing line to the Lord's Prayer. "Thine is the kingdom and the power and the glory forever." It's the Easter Entry.

John Masefield wrote a play titled *Good Friday*. At the end of the first act the crucifixion has been completed and a

"Madman" comes on stage. Speaking to a friend he says, "Friend, it is over now./The passion, the sweat, the pains,/Only the truth remains . . . ."[1] That's what these women saw, the truth. Resurrection! Then they knew it! "Thine is the kingdom, and the power and the glory forever."

So, our ancestors in the faith added this line to our Lord's prayer and we continue to say it. Does this Easter Entry make any difference to you? Does this doxology of hope, of Easter joy, fill you with new life and hope? They have made a difference to many people.

They made a difference to one of John Donne's friends. After they buried the body of John Donne in the ground one of his many admirers wrote these words with a piece of coal over his grave:

> *Reader! I am to let thee know,*
> *Donne's body only lies below;*
> *For, could the grave his soul comprise,*
> *Earth would be richer than the skies!*[2]

This Easter entry also made a difference to Dietrich Bonhoeffer. You remember him. He was the German preacher who was a part of the underground church during the Second World War, and just before the end of that war Hitler had him hanged. When they came to his prison cell to take him out for execution, Dietrich turned to a fellow prisoner and gave him a message to give to his trusted English friend, Bishop Bell. This is what he said: "Tell him that for me this is the end, but also the beginning."[3]

And these words, "thine is the kingdom and the power and the glory for ever," do make a difference to some of us. Years ago I went to see a friend of mine who was dying. She was a member of the church I was serving. She was young, the mother of two small children. In many ways it was a tragedy, but I want to tell you about my last visit with her. It took place within 24 hours of her death. As I sat by her hospital bed, she told me a funny story. In fact it was such a funny story that we both laughed so hard that I was afraid the nurses were going to throw me out of the hospital. Both of us laughed until we cried.

During that visit she also told me that before she died she wanted to be moved over into the bed next to the window. She wanted to be close to the light, the air, the outside. And later that day she was moved over next to that very window. As my visit came to a close, we prayed together, hugged one another and I left. I will never forget it.

From the time she was a little girl she had been praying the Lord's Prayer. She was reared in her church and she loved the Lord. Week after week after week she had gathered together with God's people and said the Lord's Prayer which always ended with the Easter Entry, "For thine is the kingdom and the power and the glory forever." When it came time for her to die, she understood the fullness of those words. They had been born in the resurrection of Christ and they gave her resurrection hope.

Do these words do that for you? Are they just words that were added to our Lord's prayer or do they trumpet in the good news of Easter to you? Christ is risen! All hail the power of Jesus' name. "For thine is the kingdom and the power and the glory forever. Amen!"

---

1. Quoted in *The Pulpit Digest,* March 1972, p. 33.

2. John Donne, *Devotions* (Ann Arbor: The University of Michigan Press, 1969), p. 2.

3. Mary Bosanquet, *The Life and Death of Dietrich Bonhoeffer* (New York: Harper and Row, 1968), p. 277.

A Prayer Of Confession

O God of might and mercy,
   we confess that we are slow to accept
   your power and love in our lives.
We know that you are the God of all creation,
   and yet we are slow to acknowledge your creative power.
We know that you love us intimately,
   and yet at times we are confused by the depth
   of your grace and mercy.
We know that you are always with us,
   and yet we are reluctant to accept your omnipresence.
O divine creator, draw us into your mystery
   and reshape us with your power, love and presence.
In the name of Jesus, the Christ, we pray. Amen.

OUR LORD'S PRAYER

Two Images Of The Father

"Our Father who art in heaven" .... How many times have we said these words? For some of us they seem as old as life itself. We said them around the table at home, standing by the desk at school and sitting in our Sunday school classrooms at church. Our Father who art in heaven ....

In this opening phrase of the Lord's Prayer, Jesus immediately lifts our thinking beyond the earth and into the heavens. The Father to whom we pray is sovereign, high and lifted up. Our Father is the Lord of the heavens. The word heaven is derived from an old Anglo-Saxon word "heave-on" which means to be lifted up or uplifted. Therefore, heaven is a place or state lifted above the commonplace of earth.

So the first image we get of our God is one of stateliness. This is the God whom Isaiah experienced in the temple when he wrote, "I saw the Lord sitting upon a throne, high and lifted up; and his train filled the temple" (Isaiah 6:1b). This God was surrounded by mysterious angels who broke into song, singing, "Holy, holy, holy is the Lord of hosts ..." (Isaiah 6:3b). This is a holy and mysterious God who is lifted above the commonplace of earth.

This is the God whom the psalmist envisioned when he wrote:

> *The voice of the Lord is powerful,*
> *   the voice of the Lord is full of majesty.*
> *The voice of the Lord breaks the cedars,*
> *   the Lord breaks the cedars of Lebanon.*
> *The voice of the Lord flashes forth flames of fire.*
> *The voice of the Lord shakes the wilderness,*
> *   The Lord shakes the wilderness of Kadesh.*
> *The voice of the Lord makes the oaks to whirl,*
> *   and strips the forest bare;*
> *   and in His temple all cry, "Glory!"*
> *The Lord sits enthroned over the flood;*
> *The Lord sits enthroned as king for ever.*
>
> — Psalm 29 (selected verses)

Isn't this the first image that Jesus gives us of the Father to whom he prays? This is the Father who is king, who is majestic, who is high and lifted up, who is omnipotent. This is the God who not only spat out the seven seas but the one who rules over them. This is the God who not only carved out the jagged mountains but the one who rules over them. This is the God who not only jeweled the night sky with stars and moon but the one who rules over them. This is the God who not only created the millions of life cells but the one who rules over them. This is the mighty and majestic creator of heaven and earth.

I have come to see this image of God more clearly in the first story of creation. As we read through this story in the first chapter of Genesis, we meet a God who, like a general, shouts out the orders for creation. This creator is the mighty one who just gives the orders and creation unfolds like a ripened rosebud. Hear the story. God said, "Let there be light"; and there was light. God said, "Let there be a firmament in the midst of the waters, and let it separate the waters from the waters." And God called the firmament Heaven ... God said, "Let the waters under the heavens be gathered together into one place, and let the dry land appear" (Genesis 1 — selected verses). It happened on command.

Then this majestic and powerful God called for the creation of the lights in the heavens, for the creation of the creatures of the sea, for the creation of the animals of the land and finally for the creation of human beings. The creator just gave the command and it happened. All of creation unfolded on command. This Creator-God is majestic, high, lifted up, mysterious and sovereign. And Jesus gives us this cameo shot of God when he says to pray like this: "Our Father who art in heaven." This holy one is above the commonplace of earth.

But in this same phrase, Jesus gives us another image of our God. Jesus begins the prayer with the words, "Our Father." The word translated as Father is "abba" and it is the Aramaic word which describes an intimate relationship. Many suggest that the best translation of abba is "daddy." It is a term of endearment. It breathes intimacy. So when Jesus teaches us to call God Father, he is telling us that this high and mighty one is also the close and intimate one. This Father has feeling and love and concern for each child. This Father's eye is on the sparrow and on you and me. The great God who rules over the starry heavens reaches out in love to you and me as a "daddy." What a beautiful and different image of God.

I have learned to see this image of God more clearly in the second story of creation. Creation two is very different from creation one. Here we see an intimate, loving, "hands-on" God. Hear how this creator works: "then the Lord God formed man of dust from the ground, and breathed into his nostrils the breath of life; and man became a living being" (Genesis 2:7). Do you hear the difference?

This is the God given to us in the imagery of James Weldon Johnson when he wrote that God was

*like a mammy bending over her baby,
Kneeled down in the dust
Toiling over a lump of clay
Till he shaped it in his own image;*

*Then into it he blew the breath of life,
And man became a living soul.*[1]

There is a difference. In the second story of creation we are introduced to a "hands-on" God. This Creator is our Father, our Daddy. Here is the one who has breathed into us the breath of life.

Jesus knew this God. In all of the Old Testament, God is infrequently referred to as one's personal Father. In fact, it's only seven times. All other Old Testament references to God as Father are in terms of God being the Father of a people or a nation. But Jesus refers to God as his personal Father more than 70 times in the four Gospels. He believed that God personally knew him and loved him. It was to this personal and loving God that Jesus spoke from the cross. When his body was wracked by the pains of death, Jesus said, "Father into thy hands I commit my spirit (Luke 23:46). His Father (Daddy) had not abandoned him and would not. As it was with Jesus, so it is with you and me.

If you have been fortunate enough to have had an earthly father who was a kind, personal and affectionate person, then you know of whom Jesus was speaking when he called God, Father.

In the opening line of this well-known prayer, Jesus lifts up two great images of God for us. In one we see God as majestic, holy and sovereign and in the other we see God as close and intimate and personal. And don't you and I need both? Aren't there times in our lives when we need this image of a majestic, holy and sovereign God?

We need to be able to stand and sing with assurance: "He's got the whole world in His hands." There is a Holy God in heaven who made it all and rules over it all. There is a God to whom all of life makes sense. The NASA scientist Robert Jastro said, "The motions of the galaxies, the laws of thermodynamics and the life story of the stars leads to one inevitable conclusion that this universe had a beginning with a supernatural cause and that we as scientists are learning now what the theologians have known for centuries."[2] Yes, we need the security of this majestic and sovereign God.

Natalie Barber, a college student, told about her lack of belief in God and how that changed one day when she studied the heartbeat of a 44-hour-old chicken. As the heart in the embryo began to beat and push the blood, she said, "At that moment, a new life began for me. I felt the guiding hand of God upon His universe."[3]

There are times when you and I need to feel the guiding hand of our creator upon the universe and that's one of the cameo shots that Jesus gives us of God. Our Father in heaven rules over the universe.

But we also need the other image of God, don't we? We need a God who is close and personal and intimate. We need a "Divine Daddy." Regardless of the merits of your biological father, he is not or was not able to meet all your needs. It's a real world and sometimes we feel like a fatherless child. Dick Gregory knew this feeling well and told the following personal story from his childhood.

> It was on a Thursday, the day before the Negro payday. The eagle always flew on Friday. The teacher was asking each student how much his father would give to the Community Chest. On Friday night, each kid would get the money from his father, and on Monday he would bring it to the school. I decided I was going to buy me a Daddy right then. I had money in my pocket from shining shoes and selling papers, and whatever Helene Tucker pledged for her Daddy I was going to top it. And I'd

hand the money right in. I wasn't going to wait until Monday to buy me a Daddy.

I was shaking, scared to death. The teacher opened her book and started calling out names alphabetically.

"Helene Tucker?"

"My Daddy said he'd give two dollars and fifty cents."

"That's very nice, Helene. Very, very nice indeed."

That made me feel pretty good. It wouldn't take too much to top that. I had almost three dollars in dimes and quarters in my pocket and held onto the money, waiting for her to call my name. But the teacher closed her book after she called everybody else in the class.

I stood up and raised my hand.

"What is it now?"

"You forgot me."

She turned toward the blackboard. "I don't have time to be playing with you, Richard."

"My Daddy said he's ..."

"Sit down, Richard, you're disturbing the class."

"My Daddy said he'd give ... fifteen dollars."

She turned around and looked mad. "We're collecting this money for you and your kind, Richard Gregory. If your Daddy can give fifteen dollars you have no business being on relief."

"I got it right now, I got it right now, my Daddy gave it to me to turn in today, my Daddy said ...."

"And furthermore," she said, looking right at me, her nostrils getting big and her lips getting thin and her eyes opening wide, "we know you don't have a Daddy."

Helene Tucker turned around, her eyes full of tears. She felt sorry for me. Then I couldn't see her too well because I was crying too.[4]

Sometimes we feel like a fatherless child. It may not be as graphic as Dick Gregory's experience, but it happens. Then comes Jesus' image of God. Our Father, our God, is like a "Divine Daddy" who loves us even into the next life.

James W. Angell tells the story of his first taste of death. His pet dog, a fox terrier, was struck by a car and killed. He found it in the evening by the side of the road and when he broke the news to his family his dad suggested that they leave the body in a vacant lot under cover until morning. Then he said that they would give him a proper burial.

The next morning young Jim delivered his *Des Moines Register* in the rain. He finished his paper route about 6 o'clock, and soaked with rain he went to the vacant lot to mourn over his dog. Kneeling in the rain-soaked earth, he did not hear his father approaching. Then suddenly he was aware that his dad was there dressed in his Big Smith overalls. His father didn't say a word but he gently touched his son. Jim says, "Since then it has always been easy to call God my Father."[5]

Sometimes we need a God who is our "Divine Daddy." And the good news is this: we have one.

---

1. James Weldon Johnson, *God's Trombones* (New York: The Viking Press, 1927), p. 20.

2. Howard Edington, *Close to His Majesty* Audio Tape, (First Presbyterian Church, Orlando, Florida, Sept. 23, 1990).

3. Natalie Barber, "Fragile Moments," *Guide Post*, August 1970, p. 13.

4. Robert A. Raines, *Soundings* (New York: Harper and Row, 1970), p. 94. Used by permission.

5. James A. Angell, *Yes Is A World* (Waco, Texas: Word Books, 1974), pp. 125-126.

A Prayer Of Confession

O God of our ancestors,
  we confess that we have sometimes
  taken your name in vain and failed to honor you.
You have given us life in a beautiful garden called earth,
  and we have trashed much of it.
You have surrounded us with beautiful brothers and sisters,
  and we have learned to hate and kill one another.
We are sorry for those times
  when we have dishonored you by scarring what is sacred.
We pray for your mercy, forgiveness and peace,
  in the name of Jesus, our Lord. Amen.

Our Lord's Prayer
Hallowed Be Thy Name

"Hallowed be thy name." How easily the words fall from our lips. Hallowed be thy name. This is a great phrase in our Lord's prayer because it is an affirmation of faith. It is our way of praising our God. It is our way of saying that God is the greatest! When we say, "Hallowed be thy name," we are saying that God's name is to be revered above every name. God is great!

One of the prayers that many of us taught our children was a table-grace beginning with the words, "God is great." Why have we taught them to pray those words? Why do we believe that God is great? If someone asked you why you believed that, how would you answer? Wouldn't you show them your biblical family tree? Wouldn't you tell them how God has related to your ancestors through the centuries? Your testimony might begin with the story of how your people went down to Egypt to get grain and through the years and a variety of events became slaves to the Pharaoh. They were drafted into the labor force, and made to work long hours in the boiling heat of the midday sun. They were stripped of their freedom and their dignity. Many of their sons were murdered, drowned in the Nile. Life was taken from them and their spirits crushed.

And God did a great thing! God called a man named Moses to set your ancestors free. God did great things to release your people from the bondage of slavery. Things so great that it is sometimes difficult to actually hear the story. Believe it or not, in an effort to free your ancestors from the shackles of slavery, God sent great suffering upon the Egyptians. God turned the Nile as red as blood. It thickened and the fish bloated and died. And that was just the beginning of the great freedom-works of God. Next came the frogs and then came the lice and then came the flies and then all the cattle broke out in boils. In an effort to free your ancestors, God then sent a hailstorm upon the Egyptians and then the locusts came to swarm over the land so that your ancestors could not even see the ground on which they stood. Then God sent a sandstorm and finally God sent a plague upon the Egyptians so that the cry of death and mourning went up from every Egyptian family.

And the slaves, your ancestors, rose up to follow Moses out of Egypt. They went forth with just the clothes on their backs. The young and old, the males and the females, the healthy and the maimed all went behind Moses. As they marched out of captivity, they came to the Red Sea, and God opened that sea for them. It opened in the middle and your ancestors marched through those columns of water. God led them out of that captivity and into the promised land of Canaan.

Isn't that a part of why you believe that God is great? It's a part of why I believe it. Because of these and other acts of God, we affirm God's greatness and pray, "Hallowed be thy name." And the good news is that our feeling about God's greatness is not limited to one story or one event. We are not a one-story people. We have many stories to tell. They are all there in our biblical family tree.

We hear it again and again. When God sent Jesus to come and live among us, we crucified him. He died and his death seemed to be the end of everything for his followers. He was dead and his ministry appeared to be finished. It was washed up on the shores of his crucifixion. His followers drifted aimlessly to safe quarters. All was lost.

Again, God did a great thing! God not only raised up Christ from the dead, but God also sent the Holy Spirit upon the followers of Jesus. You know the story. Our ancestors were gathered together in one place when suddenly there was a mighty wind from heaven that filled the whole house. And it looked as though there were tongues of fire resting on each person. It was such an incredible experience that the onlookers accused our ancestors of being drunk. They were not drunk. They were filled with God's spirit. And God brought them together in such a way that they became the church, our church!

God did a great thing. Is it any wonder that we pray, "Hallowed be thy name"? It's our affirmation of God. Out of the ashes of slavery God brought forth a community of people and led them to freedom, and out of the ashes of the crucifixion God brought forth a community of people and formed them into the church. God is the greatest! None is greater! Hallowed be God's name! It's all right there in the story of our ancestors. So we pray, "Hallowed be thy name."

Bertrand Russell said that if God ever asked him why he was such a skeptic he would say, "Sir, you did not give us enough information." Well, we have information. Our biblical family tree says it all. God has touched the lives of our people with great power.

Halford Luccock told the story of a printing error in the program of the performance of Handel's *Messiah*. In the "Hallelujah Chorus," instead of printing the words, "The Lord God Omnipotent reigneth," it was printed, "The Lord God Omnipotent resigneth." Dr. Luccock raised the question of whether that was a printing error or the work of a cynic who looking at the conditions of the world decided that God really had resigned.[1] There are people in the world who believe that God has resigned. We are not among them. We believe that the Lord God Omnipotent reigneth. God has done and is doing great things. Therefore, when we pray we say, "Hallowed be thy name." God's name is great!

You and I say and believe this but sometimes we fail to live it. Isn't that true? God's name is great and my name is not so great. God's name is great and your name is not so great. God's name is associated with perfection and our names are associated with imperfection. What a difference! In other words, you and I find it difficult to be faithful to our great God. We find it difficult to honor God's name in our lives and sometimes we don't. Isn't that a sad commentary? It causes us to look at another part of our biblical family tree.

Our father was named Adam and our mother was named Eve, and they set the stage for us. God gave them a perfect life in the garden of Eden. It was wonderful there. There was love and peace and tranquility and joy and meaning. God and Adam and Eve all loved one another. Adam and Eve honored God's name. But then something happened. Adam and Eve ate of the one tree which God had forbidden them to eat. It was flagrant disobedience. It was sin. Adam blamed the betrayal on Eve and she blamed it on the cunning snake. Regardless of the blame, it was sin. Disobedience to God is sin. It all began in our father and mother, Adam and Eve. Like these "parents" we do those things that we ought not to do and leave undone those things that we ought to do. We know this part of our story very well. We proclaim that God is great, but we do not always honor God's name in our everyday lives. At times we are hypocrites. We know that and it hurts.

Therefore, my name is often in conflict with God's name. The great German theologian, Helmut Thielicke, put it like this: "The truth is that we cannot pray the Lord's Prayer to the glory of God unless at the same time we pray it against ourselves. And he who has not yet learned to pray this prayer ... out of the depths of repentance, has not really prayed it at all."[2]

Couldn't each of us write his or her own litany of confession? Perhaps it would sound like one of these. I call God's name "holy" except in my work ethic where I burn the candle at both ends and abandon family members entrusted to my love and care. Or I call God's name "holy" except in my sex life wherein I often look upon others in lust. Or I call God's name "holy" except when it comes to my money where I gladly retreat into the waiting arms of greed and selfishness. Or I call God's name "holy" except when it comes to my eating and drinking where I subscribe to the old adage of eat, drink and be merry. Or I call God's name "holy" except in my devotional life which is a dim shadow of what I desire it to be. What is your litany of confession?

Hear Dr. Thielicke again. He wrote: "In every life there are these secrets, the dark documents that bear only our own name, and to which God would never put His name."[3] Barth put it like this: "Man can be important to man, a neighbor, friend, and helper, and yet at any moment indifferent, a stranger, enemy, and corrupter ... more a wolf than a person ... If you wish to know what is the true and final point of the petition 'Hallowed be thy name' ... then we had better focus our attention on this one thing, on the evil fact that we humans ... can be and are both everything and nothing to one another, both fellow men and wolves."[4] Imagine it: fellow men and wolves.

Some have said the same thing with a twist of humor. I remember a little ditty that went like this:

> *There was a young lady of Lynn*
> *who was deep in original sin.*
> *When they said, "Do be good,"*
> *she said, "I would if I could,"*
> *And straightway went at it again.*

Like our father and mother, Adam and Eve, we are unraveled by the snakes of temptation. With our brother Isaiah, we stand in the temple and cry out, "Woe is me! For I am lost; for I am a man of unclean lips, and I dwell in the midst of a people of unclean lips" (Isaiah 6:5). God's name is to be honored but frequently we dishonor it. And every time we sin against God, we are separated from God. What a sad commentary on our lives. It is enough to break the heart and crush the spirit.

But wait a minute! There is another name to be considered. It is the name of Jesus. It too is in our biblical family tree, our ancestry. We have thought of God's name and our names and now we think together about Jesus' name. Remember with me a part of the birth story of Jesus. When Joseph was engaged to Mary and found her to be pregnant, he was crushed. But an angel of the Lord came to him in a dream and said, "... do not fear to take Mary your wife, for that which is conceived in her is of the Holy Spirit; she will bear a son, and you shall call his name Jesus, for he will save his people from their sins" (Matthew 1:20-21). Isn't that the best news of all? We have a savior. Sinners have a savior. Our great God has sent a savior for people like you and me. Our great God has sent Jesus to heal the break, to reconcile the separation. Thanks be to God. Hallowed be God's name. By God's grace, we are not left to drown in the backwash of our own sins.

God has done the unthinkable, the unimaginable. God has sent God's own Son to be our savior. Literally, the name Jesus means, "The Lord saves." That is the good news. We have been disobedient and we have cut ourselves off from our great God, but we have a savior, a reconciler. Paul put it so clearly when he wrote, "God was in Christ reconciling the world unto himself, not counting their trespasses against them ..." (2 Corinthians 5:19). Clarence Jordan put the same text like this, "God was in Christ hugging the world unto himself." That's good news for you and me, who have frequently dishonored God's name and separated ourselves from our creator.

Recently members of our church were trying to qualify to have a foreign exchange student come and spend a year with them, and they asked me to write them a letter of recommendation. Partly in jest the husband said, "Put in a good word for us, Tom." Well, God has put in a good word for us. The word is the name of Jesus. That is God's very best word to us. That is God's great gift to us. Is it any wonder that we gather together and say, "Hallowed be thy name"?

Years ago I had a secretary who had a cat which had kittens. She was all excited about the litter of kittens and each morning she described them to me in vivid detail. Then one day she came to work upset because her father was going to drown all the kittens that she could not get someone to "adopt." She was a young lady still living at home, and since her father thought one cat was too many, a whole litter was out of the question. Well, the mother of these kittens was an old alley cat, and do you know how difficult it is to get rid of alley cats? Impossible, that's how difficult.

Anyhow, she prevailed upon me to come and take one of her kittens. I agreed to do so. I went to her house on a Saturday morning in the spring. The sun was shining and the birds were chirping and the earth was breaking open with new life. I went into her house and looked at the litter of kittens. Except for the one I chose, all were going to be drowned. They barely had their eyes open and they were making those little squeaky sounds with their mouths as they stayed close to their mother's stomach. Finally, I chose one. I reached in and pulled it out and held it in my hands. All the rest died in the river.

I named my kitten "Ticker" and took him home. He lived a wonderful life in our house. For 14 years he was fed and watered and loved and held and caressed. He was given the gift of life. He did nothing whatsoever to deserve it. With love, I reached into the litter of kittens and pulled him away from certain death and destruction. With love for you and me God has reached into our lives in Jesus Christ to save us from certain death and destruction.

And we say: "Hallowed be thy name."

---

1. Leonard Griffith, *God In Man's Experience* (Waco, Texas: Word Books, 1968), p. 173.

2. Helmut Thielicke, *Our Heavenly Father* (New York: Harper and Brothers, 1960), p. 45.

3. Ibid.

4. Jan Milic Lochman, *The Lord's Prayer* (Michigan: William B. Eerdmans Publishing Company, 1990), p. 39.

A Prayer Of Confession

Lord God,
*   even as we gather together to proclaim your greatness*
*   and celebrate your love,*
*   we know that we are often locked in a struggle with you.*
We are torn between our ways and your way,
*   our wills and your will,*
*   our kingdoms and your kingdom.*
Too frequently we have chosen our wills
*   and thereby contributed to the brokenness*
*   and pain in the world.*
O God, heal our brokenness, and bring in your kingdom,
*   through Christ, our Lord. Amen.*

Our Lord's Prayer

Thy Kingdom Come, Thy Will Be Done On Earth As It Is In Heaven

"Thy kingdom come, thy will be done on earth as it is in heaven." Two sermons could easily be developed from this text. In the first sermon the preacher would address the words, "thy kingdom come," and in the second the words, "thy will be done on earth as it is in heaven." Many scholars and preachers have chosen this approach. I have chosen to keep these two parts of the text together, however, because I believe they belong together. I believe that the second part of the text is a definition of the first part. If you want to know what the kingdom of God is, read the second part of the text. The kingdom of God is wherever the will of God is done as perfectly on earth as it is in heaven. That is where God reigns. So we address both phrases together: "thy kingdom come, thy will be done on earth as it is in heaven."

As we study this part of our Lord's prayer, let us begin with the suggestion that the kingdom of God has already come in Jesus Christ. We pray, "thy kingdom come," but we know that the kingdom has already come. Don't you believe that? Isaiah wrote, "There shall come forth a shoot from the stump of Jesse, and a branch shall grow out of his roots. And the Spirit of the Lord shall rest upon him" (Isaiah 11:1-2). Isaiah was telling us that the Lord was coming. Jesus was coming. The kingdom of God was coming.

And what did Jesus say after he came? What were the very first words of his public ministry? "The time is fulfilled, and the kingdom of God is at hand ..." (Mark 1:15). The kingdom of God came in Jesus.

One day in his travels Jesus met a band of lepers. There were ten of them. You know the story. He touched their lives and made them whole. Immediately following this compassionate act, Pharisees came to Jesus and asked him when the kingdom of God was coming. He said, "The kingdom of God is in the midst of you" (Luke 17:21). In a sense he was saying, "Look at me. Open your eyes. The kingdom is right here in front of you. I am the kingdom of God. I am the one in whom the will of God is being done on earth even as it is in heaven. In me God reigns!"

Some people saw this. Do you remember the story of the woman who anointed Jesus' body with the precious perfume? Why did she go out and buy that expensive ointment and put it on him? She did it because she was convinced that Jesus was the son of God and that in him God's perfect will was being done on earth even as it was in heaven. She did it to honor the king of the kingdom.

Blind Bartimaeus "saw" it also. You remember him. He sat outside the walls of Jericho for years begging coins from those who passed through the gates of that city. He lived in a world of darkness but he could hear. As he listened he heard great things about Jesus and then one day Jesus came to town. Bartimaeus cried out to him, "Jesus, Son of David, have mercy on me!" (Mark 10:47). Jesus heard his cry and touched his life. With that touch a shaft of light flashed through the blind beggar's world of darkness. Bartimaeus could see! There were leaves on the trees, faces behind the voices and stars in the heavens! What do you think would happen if we asked him if the kingdom of God had come in Jesus Christ? He would emphatically reassure us. Of course it had come. The blind man saw. The lame walked. The dumb spoke. The dead were raised. In Christ the perfect will of God was done on earth. The reign of God was here.

John Calvin said it like this: "When Christ could be pointed out with the finger, the Kingdom of God was opened."[1] If you want to see the kingdom, look at Jesus. If you want to describe it to others, point to Jesus. He is the one in whom the will of God was done on earth even as it is in heaven.

Therefore, when you and I pray, "thy kingdom come," we do so with the understanding that it has already come in Jesus, the Christ. In light of this you might ask why we pray "thy kingdom come." If the kingdom has already come, why do we pray for its coming? Isn't that a reasonable question? Indeed, why do we pray for the coming of the kingdom?

We pray for it because we know that the reign of God is not complete. The perfect will of God is not being done in the world where we live and move and have our being. The kingdom came in Christ but it is not complete. We live in a broken world where the will and ways of God are often foreign to us and our neighbors. How well we know that feeling.

Images of brokenness are everywhere. Last fall I experienced this in an overwhelming way. It all began when I attended a meeting in Wesley Church in Dover, Delaware. The church building is located at a major intersection in that city. It's a busy corner. When I came out of the meeting there were some 25 to 30 members of the Ku Klux Klan on the corners of that intersection. I blinked. For a moment, I could not believe my eyes. I had only seen members of the klan in the movies and in newspapers. But here they were in their long white robes and their pointed white hats. Others were dressed in more militant garb.

I confess to you that I did not know what to do. I was angry and frightened. I was not frightened for my personal safety but for the sanity of our community, our state and our nation. My car was parked diagonally across the street and I had to face these people to get to it. As I approached them, they tried to hand me their literature. With obvious disgust, I refused it. As I passed, one of them said sarcastically, "Have a nice day, Sir." I got in my car and sat for a moment before leaving. I needed to gather my thoughts and emotions. What a brutal sign that we live in a broken world. The kingdom of God came in Christ but the reign is not complete.

One would-be poet wrote:

God's plan made a hopeful beginning,
But man spoiled his chances by sinning
We trust that the story will end in God's glory
But at present the other side's winning.

(source unknown)

Sometimes it seems like that, doesn't it? Images of brokenness are all around us. On March 3rd, 1992, there were chilling pictures on the front page of *The New York Times*. One picture showed a group of students standing behind a large poster on which were printed the words, "Love life ... stop the killings!" An adjacent picture showed Mayor David Dinkins and Bill Cosby addressing a crowd of about 800 students. What was the occasion? Two high school students had recently been shot at point-blank range and killed.

One of the boys who was killed was named Ian Moore and he had written a poem titled, "Fear," and it was read at his funeral. Hear his words:

I fear death because I don't know
what will happen when I go
It is something I can't face
When I die, will I be thought about?
Will my name be shouted out?
Death will come at any time
No matter how far you're up the ladder.[2]

Here was a teenager who was so in touch with the brokenness of our world that he wrote about fear and death. As a participant in this broken world, he died in a hallway of his own high school at the tender age of 17 years. His poem was read at his funeral service. The kingdom did come in Jesus Christ but the reign is not complete. Images of brokenness are all around us.

We are so confused and broken that we have printed a stamp in honor of a person who used drugs and quite likely died of a drug overdose. Isn't that incredible? What are our young people to think? We tell them to "just say no" and then we honor a drug user with a stamp. Images of brokenness are all around us. Recently, those of us living in Delaware were so frustrated by the outrageous crimes of Steven Pennell that we killed him. Obviously, that helped to relieve some of our anger and hostility but what else did it accomplish? If the purpose of punishment is to redeem the wrongdoer, how was he redeemed? Images of brokenness are all around us.

Brokenness begins in our lives at an early age. Hear Robert L. Reddig's confession. One time when he was a little fellow, his mother gave him some peas to shell. It was one of his daily chores, but on this beautiful spring day, he was much more interested in playing baseball than in shelling peas. Since no one was watching, he mixed many of the unshelled pea pods in with the corn husks and threw a good half of his assignment into the slop pail for the hogs. Then he ran to join his friends for a game of baseball. Almost before he got there the full, unshelled pea pods floated to the top of the pail and betrayed him to his mother. He said that for him it was "no glorious home run ... only a guilty walk."[3]

How well we know the feeling. We are not foreigners to the brokenness in ourselves and in our world. The kingdom has come in Jesus but the reign is not complete. We suffer brokenness even to this hour.

As a people who have seen the reign of God in Christ and who now live in the midst of brokenness, we pray for the kingdom of God to come again. We pray for the will of God to reign supreme in us even as it reigned supreme in Jesus. Isn't that why we pray, "Thy kingdom come, thy will be done on earth as it is in heaven"? We have caught a glimpse of the kingdom in Jesus and we want God to do it again. We want God to reign in our lives, in our church and in our world. Do it again, God! Do it again! Do it in me. Do it in my church. Do it in my world. Reign supreme! That is our prayer!

Cyprian, who lived about 200 years after Jesus and was a bishop and writer in the early church, wrote instructions on the Lord's Prayer. He called this part of the prayer a "[longing] not for the kingdom of earth, but for the kingdom of heaven."[4] That's what it is; a "longing" for God to reign supreme in us so that God's will can be done on earth even as it is in heaven. In *The Ordination of a Priest,* there appears this line, "Imitate the mystery you celebrate." I interpret this to mean that the priest is to imitate the mystery of Christ, and I love the line. I often think of it when serving Holy Communion. At those times I "handle" the body of Christ and I want to imitate him. I want to imitate His life! I long to be like Him! It is a cry for grace!

In his letter to God a child said, "Dear God, I wish that there wasn't no such thing of (as) sin. I wish that there was not no such thing of (as) war. Tim, age 9."[5] Like Tim, we wish there was no brokenness, no sin, no war. And so we pray, "Thy kingdom come, thy will be done on earth as it is in heaven." We long for God's will to be done in us and in our world.

And it happens. It happens. People change. People grow. Grace wins. The kingdom comes. When John had his great vision which is preserved for us in the book of Revelation, the one who sat upon the throne said, "Behold, I make all things new" (Revelation 21:5). That happens. People are made new and groups are made new. The kingdom comes. God reigns.

Sometimes it happens quietly in the midst of us and we don't even see it. Sometimes it happens in the least expected places. But the good news is this: by God's grace, little by little God's kingdom comes. It happens in the lives of individual persons and in the life of the community as a whole.

First, hear the story of the coming of the kingdom in an individual. Max Beerbohn wrote a play titled, *The Happy Hypocrite,* and the main character in the play is a wealthy aristocrat named Lord George Hell. He was morally corrupt, evil. He was no good. He was a self-indulgent bum. He fell in love with a saintly girl and in an effort to win her hand in marriage, he covered his evil face with the mask of a saint. The young woman was deceived and married him.

They lived a beautiful and happy life together until Lord George Hell's past began to catch up with him. A woman out of his past wanted to show his true identity. In an effort to reveal that he was a scoundrel she challenged him to take off his mask. Poor Lord George had little choice. The mask was removed and wonder of wonders, beneath his mask was now the face of a saint. He had been transformed. He was a new person. The kingdom of God was coming in him.

Now, hear a story about the coming of God's kingdom in a community. Once upon a time I was assigned as the pastor of a church where there had been a serious problem which resulted in great brokenness. There were deep divisions in the church family. Members harbored incredible feelings of anger and hostility toward one another. I spent much of my first year listening to their stories of anger, frustration and hate. Some people told me pointedly that they would never return to that church family.

But through the years people changed. Nearly all have returned to the fold. Now most of them who harbored hard feelings toward one another work together and pray together and study together and worship together. They offer to help one another in times of adversity. Do you know why? Because they have been open to the spirit of God working in their midst and God, faithfully and quietly, has replaced anger with love and their wills with God's will. That's why. Isn't that a great testimony to God's grace and strength? Right where we live and worship the kingdom of God is coming. We have seen it. We have felt it.

Like Cyprian, we "long" for it to continue. So we pray, "Thy kingdom come, thy will be done on earth as it is in heaven."

---

1. Jan Milic Lochman, *The Lord's Prayer* (Michigan: William B. Eerdmans Publishing Company, 1990), p. 39.

2. *The New York Times,* March 4, 1992, p. B3.

3. Robert L. Reddig, "One Veiled View of God," *The Upper Room Disciplines,* 1992, p. 71.

4. Cyprian, *Second Discourse,* p. 40.

5. Hemple and Marshall, *Children's Letters to God: The New Collection* (New York: Workman Publishing, 1991).

A Prayer Of Confession

We confess to you, O God,
  that we sometimes take our daily bread for granted.
Separated from the mysteries of earth and farm,
  we frequently miss the miracles of seed bearing fruit.
Deliver us from human pride
  which dulls our sensitivity to your great works.
Creator God, as we accept our daily bread,
  as a sign of your grace,
  give us the grace to share it with others.
All this we ask in the name of Christ, our Lord,
  who broke bread and shared it with your people. Amen.

OUR LORD'S PRAYER

Give Us This Day Our Daily Bread

"Give us this day our daily bread." Literally this means, "God give bread." Isn't there a temptation to read this part of the prayer and conclude that we are asking God for the incidental or small things in life? Isn't it easy to see bread like that? It's such a simple thing. But I suggest to you that this is not a prayer for the routine and incidental things of life but a prayer for life itself. Bread was life and bread is life. We cannot live without food. We cannot live without bread. To offer this prayer is to pray for life itself, for the staff of life. Give us this day our daily bread. Give us this day what is needed to sustain life. We are asking for a great gift.

If you and I have any questions about the centrality of bread or the importance of bread, all we have to do is study our biblical story. From the beginning to the end, bread is one of the central themes in scripture. Why did Jacob and his tribe go down to Egypt? They went down there for bread. They were caught in the vise of a famine and had no grain. Egypt had stored up grain. Therefore, Jacob and the boys went to Egypt for bread.

The importance of bread seems obvious in the story of Jacob, but think for a moment of the book of Ruth where it might not be so obvious. I have a tendency to get caught up in the romance of this story and miss some of the details, but much of the story centers in bread. Elimelech and Naomi and their two sons left Judea where there was a famine and went down to the land of the Moabites. Why did they go? Elie Wiesel writes: "The motive was pragmatic in nature: it was easier to make a living there."[1] Why did they go? They went for bread, for the staff of life.

After the death of her husband and sons, Naomi decided to go back to her home, back to Judea. Why did she return? "She heard ... that the Lord had visited his people and given them food" (Ruth 1:6). She went back home for bread, for the staff of life. A daughter-in-law named Ruth went to Judea with her. As the story is told, Ruth fell in love with Boaz and married him. They had a son named Obed who was the father of Jesse, who was the father of King David. Some of you know the story. But how did Ruth and Boaz meet? How did this Judean man meet this Moabite woman? He met her when she was out gleaning in the field for grain. He met her when she was out collecting her daily bread.

The biblical evidence of the importance of bread is a thread running through many of its stories. It was bread that brought the prodigal son home. It was bread that the devil used to tempt Jesus in the desert. It was bread that Jesus blessed and multiplied to feed the 5,000. It was bread that Jesus broke and shared with his closest friends on the last night of his life.

Bread *was* important. Bread *is* important. We cannot live without it. When we ask God for our daily bread we are asking for one of the most important gifts possible, for health and energy and life itself. Food is central. Just before teaching the disciples to pray the Lord's Prayer, Jesus had told them "When you pray, go into your room and shut the door and pray to your Father ..." (Matthew 6:6). In Jesus' time, in most homes the only room with a door on it was the pantry, the place where vegetables and spices were stored. Jesus, knowing the importance of that room, told his disciples to go there and pray. Stand in the midst of your daily bread, your blessings, and pray.

When we ask God for our daily bread, we ask for life itself. It is a big thing, not a little thing. The Jews made it a starting point for their religion; the Romans ruled by it. In *Les Miserables,* Jean Valjean stole for it. Jesus enjoyed it so much that his enemies called him a "glutton" (Matthew 11:19). When Elie Wiesel was freed from the concentration camp at Buchenwald, he wrote, "Our first act as free men was to throw ourselves onto the provisions. We thought only of that. Not of revenge, not of our families. Nothing but bread."[2] It is one of life's necessities. It is life!

Ernest Campbell told a story about a woman who went to a pet store to buy a parrot to keep her company. She took the parrot home with great expectations, but returned to the pet shop the next day to report that the parrot had not said a word.

The storekeeper asked if the parrot had a mirror and when the woman reported that it did not have a mirror, he suggested that she buy him one. He explained that parrots liked to look at themselves in the mirror and with this added joy, the parrot would talk. She bought the mirror and went home, but the next day she returned with the same complaint. The parrot did not talk. So the storekeeper suggested that the woman buy her parrot a ladder. He explained that parrots enjoyed walking up and down ladders and perhaps this added pleasure would encourage him to talk. So she bought the ladder and went home.

Sure enough, the next day she was back again with the same complaint. The parrot did not talk. The storekeeper asked if the parrot had a swing and the woman said that he did not have a swing. The storekeeper said the parrots loved to swing and perhaps this would do the trick. So the woman took the swing and went home but the next day she returned to the store to announce that the parrot had died. The storekeeper was very sorry to hear that and asked if the parrot ever spoke a word before he died. "Oh, yes," said the lady, "it said, 'Don't they sell any food down there?' " Bread is life. Without it we die.

Therefore, when we say, "Give us this day our daily bread," we are asking God for one of the most important things known to us. We are asking for the staff of life, for life itself. It's a giant request.

And the good news is that God gives us our daily bread. We depend upon God for this source of life and God alone supplies it. Dr. J. Howard Edington called this part of the prayer "a declaration of dependence." Isn't that a good description? It is a declaration of dependence. We depend upon God to give us our daily bread, to sustain our lives. The bread on our tables is not a barometer of our success but a sign of God's grace. We learned that as children when we prayed, "By God's hand we all are fed. Give us Lord our daily bread."

In our more sane moments we know that we cannot convert the seed into grain. We cannot supply the water needed to nurture the earth. We cannot supply the sun rays that warm the earth. We are at God's mercy for our daily bread, and we have a graphic picture of this in the Old Testament.

Our Jewish ancestors stormed out of Egypt and into the wilderness with little knowledge of how difficult it would be for them to find food in the desert. And it was difficult. In fact, it was impossible. In fact, it took a miracle for them to be fed, and they experienced just such a miracle.

This beautiful story is preserved for us in the 16th chapter of Exodus. Each morning when these Exodus people awakened in the wilderness, they found little white flakes on the ground. It was called manna and it tasted like wafers made with honey. Each morning they were to collect one omer per person. That's about a half a gallon. They were not to collect any more than that. If they collected more it just rotted and became wormy. The only exception was the day before the sabbath when they were allowed to collect an extra omer per person so they would not have to work on the sabbath day. It was called "angel bread" or "heavenly bread." It was manna from heaven. It was the gift of God for the people of God. They were totally and completely dependent on God. They knew they lived by God's grace.

This is reflected in the lines of the psalmist when he wrote, "The eyes of all mankind look up to you for help; you give them their food as they need it. You constantly satisfy the hunger and thirst of every living thing" (Psalm 145:15-16). It is also reflected in this Jewish grace which comes to us from the time of Jesus: "Praised be thou, O Lord our God, king of the world, who dost feed the whole world by thy goodness. In grace, love, and mercy he gives bread to all flesh ... For he feeds and provides for all and shows his kindness to all and assigns food to all his creatures which he has made. Praised be thou, Lord, who dost feed all."[3]

Do you say grace? Have you had your breakfast? Did you say grace? Did you acknowledge that you are dependent upon God for your daily bread and that you are grateful that God supplies it? Or did you just take it for granted? In some quarters, saying grace is such an unusual thing that people are startled by it. In the *New York Times,* Joel Engel began an article about an actress with these words, "Marisa Tomei bows her head for grace before eating a sandwich ...." Isn't that a remarkable opening line of an article about an actress? Why did he mention her prayer over her sandwich? Isn't it because he thought it highly unusual? Do you say grace?

The bread on our tables is not a barometer of our success but a sign of God's grace. The last words that Martin Luther wrote before his death were: "We are beggars, that is true."[4] He wrote them on a scrap of paper. We are beggars, that is true. And God who is great feeds us beggars. God gives us food. We ask God for bread, the gift of life, and God supplies it. It's a daily miracle of grace.

In summary, bread is important and it is given to us by God. Now, a third thing needs to be said. God gives us the bread to share with one another. Notice the wording in our

Lord's prayer: "Give *us* this day *our* daily bread." Us and our are plural pronouns. Imagine the prayer reading like this: Give me this day my daily bread. Wouldn't that make all the difference in the world? Jesus chose the words "us" and "our" because God's gift of bread belongs to all of God's children. We are to share our bread.

This teaching is as old as the church itself. In the first verse of the sixth chapter of Acts we learn that some people were upset because "their widows were neglected in the daily distribution." What was the daily distribution? It was bread. In the early church bread was shared daily with the widows and the orphans.

It's not always easy to do that, is it? Addressing this petition of our Lord's prayer, Cyprian wrote, "Daniel had a meal miraculously provided, when he was shut up by the command of the king in the den of lions: and among wild beasts hungering, yet sparing him, the man of God was nourished. Thus Elijah received sustenance in his flight, and was fed through persecution, by ravens that ministered to him in his solitude, and birds that bare him meat. And oh! the horrid cruelty of human wickedness! the wild beasts spare, and the birds give food, while it is men that lurk and rage."[5]

Is he right? Do the animals and birds care more for us than we care for one another? I hope not. Recently a church member reminded the Sunday morning congregation of her church that while they were in that service almost 2,000 children would die of starvation and malnourishment-related diseases. Imagine that! That same lay person then asked those assembled to give some coins to buy these children food. Just a few coins would provide a child with a 1,300-calorie biscuit. That's the total daily bread for many children in the world. All of it! And all of this happens while many of us try to figure out ways to lose weight. All of this happens while we try to discipline our eating habits. All of this happens while many of us carefully shop for those restaurants which advertise "all you can eat!"

There is a Latin American prayer which speaks deeply to this issue: "O God, to those who have hunger give bread;

and to those who have bread, the hunger for justice."⁶ God gives the bread to be shared among all God's children. Some catch this vision in marvelous ways.

One such person is Johnny, who was a friend of mine in a previous parish. He was in his late 30s but he had the mental age of an eight- or nine-year-old. He was active in the church where he was loved and nurtured. Sometimes he had trouble sitting through an entire service, and because of that he would frequently get up and go out. Sometimes he would return and sometimes he would not. The congregation was easy with him. Everyone understood and loved Johnny.

One Sunday in the sermon I was talking about people who did not have food. I described these hungry people, and near the end of the sermon Johnny got up and left. No one thought anything about it. We went on with the service and when it was time for the offering, Johnny came back. He came in carrying a bag of groceries. He brought them up to the altar, gave them to me and said, "This is for the hungry people." There was not a dry eye in the house.

Our daily bread is a gift from God to be shared with the people of God.

---

1. Elie Wiesel, *Sages and Dreamers* (New York: Summit Books, 1991), p. 53.

2. Elie Wiesel, *Night* (New York: Bantam Books), p. 109.

3. Jan Milic Lochman, *The Lord's Prayer* (Michigan: William B. Eerdmans Publishing Company, 1990), p. 99.

4. Gerhard Ebeling, *On Prayer* (Philadelphia: Fortress Press, 1966), p. 90.

5. Cyprian, *Second Discourse,* p. 44.

6. Lochman *op. cit.,* p. 98.

A Prayer Of Confession

O God of us all,
  we are sorry for those times
  when we have acted more like animals than angels.
We confess that we have not always been humble and loving
  enough to forgive those who have hurt us.
It is easier for us to ask for your forgiveness
  than it is to forgive one another.
In your mercy, O God,
  bless us with the strength to echo
  your love and forgiveness throughout the world.
We pray in the name of Jesus, the Christ,
  who died for our forgiveness. Amen.

Our Lord's Prayer
Forgive Us As We Forgive Others

"And forgive us our trespasses as we forgive those who trespass against us." Or are we supposed to say, "Forgive us our debts as we forgive our debtors"? How many times have you been caught saying "trespasses" in the Presbyterian Church when all others were saying "debts"? In those times I feel a little like the man in the shaving commercial who cuts himself and a voice says, "Gotcha." Why do some of us say "debts" and "debtors" while others say "trespasses" and "trespass"? Have you ever thought about that? After all, the King James Version of the Bible uses the word "debt." Why should we do otherwise?

The background of this difference is all a matter of church history. One of the reasons for the protestant reformation in England in 1530 was that the people wanted the scriptures made available in English. In 1525 William Tyndale had completed an English translation of the New Testament and in doing so he used the word "trespasses." The Church of England adopted this translation and put it in their prayer book. Since John Wesley loved and used that prayer book, the Methodists and other denominations which grew out of the Wesleyan movement follow in the tradition of Tyndale and use trespasses. Perhaps it would be more exciting if there were some deeper theological explanation of this issue, but it just isn't so. It's a rather dry matter of church history.

Actually, there are quite a variety of translations of this biblical text by now. In the Weymouth translation it is "forgive us our shortcomings." In The Living Bible it is "forgive us our sins." In the Amplified Version it is "forgive us our resentments." And in the New English Bible it is "forgive us the wrong we have done."

Regardless of how the text is translated, it begins with one major assumption. We are debtors. We are trespassers. We are sinners. We have done those things that we ought not to have done and left undone those things that we ought to have done. We have been disobedient to God and disobedience to God is sin. We were created in the image of God and we have distorted that godly image. We are not what God intended us to be. We were created a little lower than the angels (Psalm 8:5 KJV) and sometimes we act as though we were created a little lower than the animals. Jesus saw right through us and taught us to pray with the assumption that we are sinners, debtors, trespassers. His assumption is that we need forgiveness and so we ask for it by praying, "Forgive us our trespasses."

Of course we are not alone in this predicament. Even our favorite biblical characters stand beside us as sinners. Peter, the big fisherman, had his dark side. You'll remember that he promised to follow Jesus to his death, but he could not do it. When Jesus was walking alone on the thorny path to crucifixion, Peter had a wonderful opportunity to bear witness to him, but he denied that he ever knew Jesus. Furthermore, he denied it with an oath. He cursed. He felt so badly about what he had done that he went off by himself and cried like a baby. Oh yes, Peter stands beside us as a sinner. If you can imagine it, even Paul had his dark side. Perhaps he gave one of the best summaries of our predicament when he said, "For I do not do the good I want, but the evil I do not want is what I do" (Romans 7:19). Oh yes, the great apostle Paul stands beside us as a sinner.

But isn't it sometimes difficult for us to accept the label of sinner? A friend told me a story about little Mary who was a bad girl and consequently her mother told her to go to her room and pray to God for forgiveness. She obeyed her mother and did as requested. When she came out of her room her mother asked, "Did you ask God to forgive you?" "Oh yes," said Mary, "and God said, 'Mercy me, little Mary, I know heaps worse'n you.' "[1]

Don't you sometimes feel like that? Don't you know heaps worse'n you? I know heaps worse'n me. Through such comparisons it's easy for us to be comforted into the place where we conclude that we are not really sinners, that we are debt-free. In our more sane moments, don't we know better? In fact, don't we sometimes scare ourselves? Knowing what we have done and what we have thought about doing causes us to worry about what we might be capable of doing. Isn't it scary? None of us is positively certain of just how dark our dark side might be.

Jesus, seeing perfectly into the human heart, begins with the assumption that we are sinners in need of forgiveness. Rudolf Bohren claims that this petition for forgiveness belongs next to the petition for bread. Because as much as we need our bread, our daily bread, we need forgiveness.[2]

Before moving from this thought let's remember that our debt is not only to God but also to our fellow human beings. It is impossible to sin against God without betraying our brothers and sisters and it is impossible to sin against our brothers and sisters without betraying our God. Gerhard Ebeling wrote: "Our debts towards our neighbor and our debts towards God form one single tangle of debt."[3]

So Jesus teaches us to pray with the assumption that we are all sinners, all debtors, all trespassers. Because we are in this state, we pray to God to "forgive us." And God offers us forgiveness in Jesus Christ our Lord. Jesus comes to tell us that God's love is greater than our sin. He comes to die on a cross for us. He comes to cancel the debt.

Isn't his life filled with forgiveness? It was the heart of his preaching and the heart of his practice. His stories are lined with love and forgiveness. What is the message of the parable of the prodigal son if it is not forgiveness? A son went away and betrayed his father, himself and his brother, and when he came home again, the father welcomed him back with forgiveness. He met him in the field and fell on him and hugged and kissed him and called for a party to be given. Forgiveness!

Jesus did not just preach it; he practiced it. They brought an adulteress to him. There was no question about her crime since she was caught in the very act. And what did Jesus do for her? He forgave her and gave her another chance. He set her free from those who would have stoned her to death. He also set her free from herself and her own condemnation. He practiced what he preached. Forgiveness!

Emerson said, "His heart was as great as the world, but there was no room in it to hold the memory of a wrong." Isn't that so true? When John Killinger wrote a sermon on this petition of our Lord's prayer he titled it, "A Festival of Forgiveness."[4] The story of Jesus is a festival of forgiveness. From the woman in the streets to the criminal on the cross, from the disciple who lied about him to the disciple who doubted his resurrection, from the tax collector who robbed the people to the paralytic who could not walk, the message was the same: your sins are forgiven. His story is a festival of forgiveness. It is the story of slates wiped clean. It is the story of second chances and new beginnings. In one last, loving act Jesus died on the cross to cancel our debts, to forgive our sins.

Do you know what it is like to be saddled with a great debt? Many of you have lived through those times and some of you may be living through them now. If we are saddled with great debts, it makes a difference in how fully we can live. It makes a difference in how often we can go out for entertainment and enjoyment. It makes a difference in how much we can give to others. It makes a difference in how much and how far we can travel. It makes a difference in what we eat and where we live. It makes a difference in health care and educational opportunities. To be saddled with a great debt is to be limited in life. To have the debt canceled is to be set free to live more fully. Jesus said that he came to bring us abundant life, to help us live more fully. When he cancels our debts, forgives our sins, he sets us free to live more fully.

Does this mean we are now perfect? Does this mean that we sin no more? Does this mean that Jesus is like a 20th century chemical that cleanses us for the rest of our lives? Of course it doesn't mean that. It simply means that my sins no longer separate me from my God. The power of God's love is greater than our sins that would separate us from one another. In Christ God has canceled my debt. Christ is the drum major in the festival of forgiveness!

We need forgiveness. God gives forgiveness. And a third thing needs to be said. We are called to forgive others. The miracle of forgiveness is not a line between God and me, but it is a cycle which includes God, me, and my brothers and sisters. As I receive it, I share it with others. It is a cycle. Isn't that obvious in the prayer? Jesus taught us to pray saying, "Forgive us our trespasses as we forgive those who trespass against us." It is all interconnected. It is a cycle of forgiveness. No one is exempt. As we have our debts canceled, we cancel the debts of others. As we are forgiven, we forgive others. We pass it on.

Recall Jesus' parable of the unforgiving servant. It is about the cycle of forgiveness. A wealthy man was settling his accounts with his servants. He called in one of his servants who owed him much money. The wealthy man asked for his money and since the poor man could not pay it, he ordered the poor man to be sold along with his wife and children and all that they owned. This was to be done to partially pay the debt. The poor servant fell on his knees and begged for mercy. And out of pity for him the wealthy man released him and forgave him his debt. Isn't that a beautiful story? It is, but that is not the end of the story. Don't applaud yet.

This same servant went out and met another servant who owed him money and he demanded full payment. This poor fellow servant could not pay the debt and he begged for mercy. But the servant who had just been forgiven of his debt refused to forgive the one indebted to him. In fact he had him thrown into prison.

This story got back to the wealthy man who had forgiven the servant of his debt. Hearing what had happened he ordered the forgiven servant to come back and see him. The wealthy man said to him, "You wicked servant! I forgave you all that debt because you besought me; and should not you have had mercy on your fellow servant, as I had mercy on you?" And in anger he sent him off to jail (Matthew 18:32f).

What happened? The cycle was broken! We forgive others as we have been forgiven, or we break the cycle and that line of grace grinds to a halt. Is someone waiting for your forgiveness? Is someone just waiting for you to say the word, to set them free, to continue the cycle? Is it a husband or wife who has betrayed you? Is it a brother who has not spoken to you for years? Is it a parent who used you? Is it an employer who lied to you? Is it a neighbor who unjustly criticized your child? Is there anyone anywhere waiting for your forgiveness? Are you in danger of breaking the cycle?

Helmut Thielicke said, "We are all echoes. The only question is echoes of what?"[5] He goes on to say that we are either echoes of hatred and harshness and injustice or we are echoes of Christ and his grace, love and forgiveness. Have you ever thought of yourself as an echo? If so, what are you echoing? Is it hate and revenge or is it love and forgiveness?

Isn't it easy to drift into being an echo of hate and revenge? Don't you know that tug, that pull? I was having a lively discussion with several acquaintances about basketball. Suddenly one of the men, referring to the blacks, said, "Those spooks can really jump." It's so easy to echo hatred and prejudice.

Sometimes it's subtle, but other times it is strident. Will Campbell had one of his relatives tell him how he felt about another person. This is what he said, "You know, Wee Willie, I don't hate anybody. 'Cause the Bible says it's a sin to hate. But there are some folks I hope dies of cancer of the tonsils."[6]

Some people echo revenge and hate, and they break the cycle of forgiveness. But there are others who echo Christ's love and forgiveness and they continue the cycle of forgiveness.

Years ago in another parish, I had a friend die. He was one of the fine members of the church I was serving. I had spent many hours with him during the final days and hours of his sickness. He had cancer and death came to him in slow motion. Since I had been so deeply involved with him and other members of his family, I thought I knew all about his family. When he died I met with his wife and children to plan a memorial service and in that meeting discovered that he had a brother. I was amazed. I had never seen his brother or heard of his brother. His brother had never visited, called or written during these months of illness. The wife then explained to me that the brothers were estranged. Her husband and the brother had not seen or spoken to one another for years.

I asked her if he would attend the service and she assured me that he would not. So we planned the service as though the brother did not exist. No mention was to be made of his name.

We gathered together for the service and all was going well. As usual, near the end of the service I asked if there were any people who would like to rise and give witness to the life of the deceased. Since he had been so active in the church, several stood to bear witness. Then a man I did not know rose in the back of the room and walked toward the front. He was well dressed and he came right up to the lectern where I was standing. He wanted to use the microphone. He wanted to be heard.

He began his remarks by telling us that he was a brother to the deceased and that their worlds had followed different tracks and their relationship had come apart. He said that he was sorry for his part in that separation and he wanted to offer forgiveness and be forgiven. It was an incredible moment. As he left the chancel area to go back to his seat, the widow, his sister-in-law, and her children all rose to greet him warmly. They all hugged and kissed him.

It was the cycle of forgiveness in living color, and we all got to see it. What an echo of love and grace! What an echo! It still rings in my heart!

---

1. From a paper, "Management As A Profession," by Mary Parker Follett, October, 1925.

2. Jan Milic Lochman, *The Lord's Prayer* (Michigan: William B. Eerdmans Publishing Company, 1990) p. 107.

3. Gerhard Ebeling, *On Prayer* (Philadelphia: Fortress Press, 1966), p. 101.

4. John Killinger, *The God Named Hallowed* (Nashville: Abingdon Press, 1988), p. 53.

5. Helmut Thielicke, *Our Heavenly Father* (New York: Harper and Brothers, 1960), p. 113.

6. Will D. Campbell, *Brother to a Dragon Fly* (New York: Continuum, 1977), p. 181.

A Prayer Of Confession

Lord God,
    we confess that it is difficult
    to keep you central in our lives.
Great temptations come to tarnish your image
    and to pull us away from you.
We are locked in a daily struggle to be your faithful and
    obedient people, and sometimes we feel weak.
We cry out to you for grace, O God.
Strengthen us for our times of trial
    and stand by us as we face the tempter.
In the holy name of Christ, our Lord, we pray. Amen.

Our Lord's Prayer
Lead Us Not Into Temptation But Deliver Us From Evil

I thought it was going to be a routine hospital visit. I pulled up a chair and began to talk with this friend who was in his early 60s. Our conversation became deep and involved. This man did not feel good about his life or about his relationship to God. From time to time tears filled his eyes. Then he asked me to get his wallet out of a drawer and hand it to him. I did that, and he "fished" around in the wallet until he finally pulled out a picture. He handed me the picture.

It was a picture of Jesus but it was so faded that it was almost unrecognizable. He told me that the picture was a good description of what had happened to his relationship to the Lord. It had faded. He told me that once that picture had been clear just as his faith in Christ had been clear. But now his faith, like the picture, was faded. Somehow the Lord had faded from his life. What an image.

That's the subject of this petition of our Lord's prayer: "Lead us not into temptation but deliver us from evil." This is about the temptations that come to you and me to move our Lord out of the center of our lives. It's about the temptations that dull the image of our Lord. It's about those things in life that come to separate us from our Heavenly Father.

Helmut Thielicke preached on this passage in his native Germany after the Second World War and this is what he said: "This is exactly what temptation means: to allow oneself to be torn away from God. And here again we must not think in terms of peccadilloes and 'puppy-sins'; we must not equate temptation with a child's urge to 'snitch' or our temptation to stay in bed or to show up late for work. No, temptation has to do with something totally different. It is actually the fact that through small and great events in our life, little fondnesses and great passions, we can be brought to the point where we lose contact with the Father."[1]

When you and I pray, "Lead us not into temptation but deliver us from evil," we are praying that the presence of Christ will not dull in our lives. We are praying that we will not be torn away from our creator God.

Think for a moment about some of the forms of temptation that threaten to tear us away from our God, to drive a wedge between us and our Lord. What comes to your mind? Aren't catastrophes a form of temptation that threaten to separate us from our God? Isn't that what tore Judas away from Christ? When Judas signed up as one of Jesus' disciples, Christ was the very center of his life. He was so much the center, that Judas left everything to follow after him. Then came a catastrophe. Jesus was going to go off and die on a cross. He was not going to run the Roman army into the sea and set up the kingdom envisioned by Judas. Judas was not going to become the Secretary of the Treasury of this new kingdom. Judas decided that he had made a mistake. He had left everything and placed all his bets on a loser. And Judas lost all perspective. This catastrophe in Judas' life pushed the Christ right off center stage. His picture of the Christ dulled and dulled and dulled. The disciple was separated from his master. Yes, temptations sometimes come in the form of catastrophes which threaten to tear us away from God.

I experienced this in a previous parish where there was a man who attended church every Sunday even though he did not believe in God. He came with his wife. One spring day I went out to visit him. The world was alive with the sights and sounds and smells of new life. He was a great gardener and we sat out in his flower garden. It was there that he decided to tell me his story. He had once been a pillar in the church. He had held high offices and been very, very faithful. He was close to his God.

Then one day their baby daughter got sick. They rushed her to the hospital and she became critically ill. He and his wife decided that she would spend the night and he would go home and rest. Then the next day he would stay with the child while his wife went home to rest. So he went home and before going to bed he prayed for his baby daughter. He wanted her to live more than he had ever wanted anything in his whole life. When he finished praying he said that the whole room was filled with peace. He seemed to be in a sea of peace. God was there for him and he was convinced that the child would live. That night she died, and with her death came the death of Christ in this man's life. It was this catastrophe, this death of his firstborn child, that tore him away from his Lord.

Yes, catastrophes are one form of temptation that threaten to tear us away from our Lord, and some suffer to that end. It's a big bang and they never recover. But others are separated from God in more subtle ways. They just drift away. It's like erosion. The picture of Christ dulls with the passage of time. There is no great catastrophe. In fact, these people really can't put their finger on any specific time or event. They don't know exactly when it was that they got separated from the Lord. They just know that their stories are filled with the words "used to." They "used to" believe. They "used to" feel close to God. They "used to" have a good relationship with Christ. They "used to" worship in the church. They "used to" pray. "Used to . . ." What an icy epitaph.

They got separated gradually, with the passage of time. If pressed, some of these people may take a guess at when it all began. Some explain that it probably started when they bought a place at the beach. That place took so much time and energy that the Lord began to fade. Others explain that it probably started when the kids got involved in sports and those weekend activities cut the church right out of the picture. The Lord God began to fade. Others explain that it all began when the wife went to work and suddenly the household chores took more time and energy. The Lord God began to fade. Still others explain that it probably started when the kids grew up and they no longer did church things as a family. The Lord God began to fade.

For all such persons, separation from God came gradually. It was like the erosion of the sand into the sea. Day by day the picture of Christ faded more and more and more until he was hardly recognizable. There was no great catastrophe, just daily erosion.

Irving Feldman writes this line in one of his poems: "The mugger messages come for my soul,/pressing their hot slogans to my throat,/whispering, 'Give it to us, give it to us.' "[2] How well we know the "mugger" and the whisper.

Sometimes the tempter comes to tear us away from God with the crash of a catastrophe and other times with the whisper of the mugger. Sometimes it's because of a great event and other times it's because of gradual erosion.

Because we know the power of temptation and evil, we cry out to God for the grace to stay close to our Lord. We say it boldly, "Lead us not into temptation but deliver us from evil." It is a cry for help from on high.

Where do we find help? What are our sources of grace needed to overcome temptations? I suggest that we look at the life of Christ to see his sources of grace when he was faced with temptation.

When Christ was tempted in the wilderness, God's word was a source of grace and strength. Have you ever noticed that? You know the story. Jesus was driven out into the wilderness and there he was tempted by the devil. First the devil tempted Jesus to turn stone into bread. And how did Jesus respond? He quoted scripture from Deuteronomy. He said to the devil, "Man shall not live by bread alone, but by every word that proceeds from the mouth of God" (Matthew 4:4). The devil hardly missed a beat before inviting Jesus to throw himself off the pinnacle of the temple so the angels could bear him up and save him. What did Jesus do? Again, he quoted scripture from Deuteronomy by saying, "You shall not tempt the Lord your God" (Matthew 4:7). Then the devil took Jesus to a very high mountain and showed him all the kingdoms of the world and promised that all of these could be his if he just bowed down and worshiped him. What did Jesus do? For the third time, he quoted scripture from Deuteronomy and said, "You shall worship the Lord your God and him only shall you serve" (Matthew 4:10).

When Jesus was tempted, he called on the word of God. For him scripture was a form of grace. It was a form of grace that strengthened him to stand against the tempter. The word of God is a channel of grace for us also!

During the First World War the great theologian Paul Tillich was in a division of the German army that was in heavy fighting. He wrote to his father, "Hell rages around us. It's unimaginable."[3] He was in emotional and mental anguish as he was caught up in this inferno of death. Tillich said that what helped to keep him from being torn apart from his God was that great line of Paul's which he kept repeating to himself, "For I am sure that neither death, nor life, nor angels, nor principalities, nor things present, nor things to come, nor powers, nor height, nor depth, nor anything else in all creation, will be able to separate us from the love of God in Christ Jesus our Lord" (Romans 8:38-39).[4]

Like his Lord, Tillich found grace in Holy Scripture. It was a source of strength in his life. No doubt many of you have similar stories.

When Jesus faced temptation, he did not only depend on God's word for strength, but he also depended on prayer. For him prayer was also a channel of grace. On the night before his death, he was faced with great temptation. It was his will against God's will. How well we know the struggle. Jesus went into the Garden of Gethsemane to pray.

You have seen pictures of this great moment in his life many times. He knelt there in the Garden of Gethsemane to pray his way through the struggle. It was the battle of the "cups." Not my "cup" but yours! No! Not your "cup" but mine! My "cup"! Your "cup"! In this struggle to do God's will, prayer was a channel of grace for Christ. In prayer he found the strength to rise above the temptation. In all of this Jesus was simply practicing what he preached when he said, "Watch and pray, that you may not enter into temptation; the spirit indeed is willing, but the flesh is weak" (Matthew 26:41). Prayer is a channel of grace for us also.

Because his life story was told to us in the film, *A Man For All Seasons*, many of us know something about the life of Sir Thomas More. One time his friends warned him about his health and suggested that he not rise so early in the morning day after day after day for his prayers and communion. Sir Thomas More replied to his friends, "I have so many decisions each day; I have so many distractions and temptations, that I could not survive each day unless I received my Lord, my God, and my Heavenly King."[5] He couldn't make it without prayer.

Like his Lord Jesus Christ, Sir Thomas More was convinced that prayer was a channel of grace in his life. It was one of the ways that God funneled strength to him so that he would not succumb to the "mugger," the evil one. Don't we know that feeling? Isn't the same true for us? In prayer we open our hearts to the very one we are trying to stay close to and God ministers to us.

There is a third and final source of grace that Jesus used to fight temptation. In addition to scripture and prayer, he found strength in his friends. When Jesus went to the Garden of Gethsemane he took his friends with him. He asked Peter, James and John, his three closest friends, to go into the deepest part of the garden with him. You may want to argue that they didn't seem to offer much help since they slept while he struggled with temptation. I agree that they slept, but they were there. His friends were there. They did not fully understand, but they were there. Friends never ever fully understand our personal trials and temptations but their presence can be a great source of strength.

Aristotle said, "In poverty and other misfortunes of life, true friends are a sure refuge. — The young they keep out of mischief . . ." There is strength in friends. They help to keep us from being torn away from our Lord.

Isn't that true of Alcoholics Anonymous? Why do they gather together with their friends? Friends provide strength and support. With our friends around us we are more likely to rise above the temptations that threaten to tear us from God.

Maurice Baring wrote these words about his friend:

> *Because of you we will be glad and gay,*
> *Remembering you, we will be brave and strong;*
> *And hail the advent of each dangerous day,*
> *And meet the last adventure with a song.*[6]

One of the most incredible stories of friendship I have ever heard comes from C. S. Lewis. He married late in life and in his wife he found the fullest perfection of love. Their friendship was deep and dear. Then she got cancer and started that long, slow journey toward death. C. S. Lewis explained that it was then that he accepted her pain. He said that the pain actually left her body and entered into his body. He felt her pain in his body, literally! Lewis said, "It was crippling. But it relieved hers."[7]

As you and I struggle to stay close to our Lord, we cry out for help. We cry out to God for grace. We say, "Lead us not into temptation but deliver us from evil." And Jesus reminds us of our weapons. The three sources of grace that helped him in his time of trial were the word of God, prayer and his friends.

These are also channels of grace for you and me.

---

1. Helmut Thielicke, *Our Heavenly Father* (New York: Harper and Brothers, 1960), pp. 119-120.

2. Irving Feldman, "The Flight of The City," *All of Us Here* (New York: Viking Press, 1986), p. 67.

3. Wilhelm and Marion Pauck, *Paul Tillich, His Life and Thoughts, Vol. 1* (New York: Harper and Row, 1976), p. 49.

4. *Ibid.*

5. John J. Ahern, *Eight Happy People* (Milwaukee: Bruce Publishing Co., 1964), p. 35.

6. Rita F. Snowden, *The Time of Our Lives* (Nashville: Abingdon Press, 1966), p. 192.

7. William Barclay, *Daily Celebration, Vol. 2* (Waco, Texas: Word Books, 1973), p. 81.

www.ingramcontent.com/pod-product-compliance
Lightning Source LLC
Chambersburg PA
CBHW071756040426
42446CB00012B/2580